KNOCK

Julia A. Royston

BK
ROYSTON
Publishing

BK Royston Publishing
Jeffersonville, IN 47131
http://www.bkroystonpublishing.com
bkroystonpublishing@gmail.com

Cover Design: BK Royston Publishing
Cover Photo: Jonathan Snorten

ISBN-13: 978-1-967282-28-9

Printed in the United States of America

Dedication

Ideas are great.

Research is necessary.

Success begins when you actually go forth and **Knock** on that first door of opportunity.

Theme Scripture

Ask, and it shall be given you;
Seek, and ye shall find;

Knock, and it shall be

opened unto you:

Matthew 7:7 (KJV)

Acknowledgements

I thank my Lord and Savior Jesus Christ for giving me another opportunity to introduce more people to you. I thank you for entrusting this gift to me. Lord, let your Spirit move, guide and empower through this book to the people who will read it.

To my husband, Brian K. Royston, the love of my life, for loving and cheering me on so much that I can be and do all that God has placed in me. I love you.

To my mom, my greatest supporter and best friend. To my dad, who is in Heaven, who I know is proud of me and always encouraged me to go for it. Thanks to all the rest of my family for their love and support.

A special thank you to Rev. and Mrs. Claude R. Royston for their love and support.

To the rest of my clients, friends and family, thank you and love you always.

Let's go!

Table of Contents

Introduction

This is Part 3 of the scripture Matthew 7:7 and the third devotional in this particular series. It's time to Knock. This part is even harder for people who need all of the money, know exactly who to call, and have a problem with rejection. The first door that you knock on doesn't always open for you, and most of the time, the first door is a no. But you have to keep finding more doors and keep knocking. The right door for you will open. The right opportunity will come for you at the right time but definitely won't come if you don't get up, go to the door and knock.

Even Jesus is standing at the door of your heart, knocking. He is waiting for you to open the door for Him to come in. You can pray, you can fast, you can ask, you can seek, but until you open the door for the person who is knocking, the answer won't come.

The person who asks will get what they need. The person who seeks will find what they seek. For the person who actually goes to the door and knocks, the door will be opened.

Ask. Seek. Knock.

Let's go!

He's Knocking

"Look! I have been standing at the door, and I am constantly knocking. If anyone hears me calling him and opens the door, I will come in and fellowship with him and he with me."

Revelation 3:20 (TLB)

As much as we actually say that we're waiting on God, He's actually waiting on us. For what, you ask? For you to open the door and let Him in. Have you ever gone to someone's house and knocked on the door but they didn't hear it or want to hear it and they eventually never came to the door to open it? Once, I had something great to give someone, but they didn't open the door so I took the gift and went home. In Revelations, He says that He is constantly knocking, not knocking one time and walking away, but He is constantly knocking. Remember that He's not a burglar or thief or invader, He must be invited in.   When invited in, He's got wonderful things to share, answers to your problems and relief for your pain, but you must open the door. Don't you hear it? Somebody's knocking at the door.

REFLECTION

_____
_____
_____
_____
_____
_____
_____
_____
_____
_____
_____
_____
_____
_____
_____
_____
_____
_____
_____
_____
_____
_____

REFLECTION

_____

_____

_____

_____

_____

_____

_____

_____

_____

_____

_____

_____

_____

_____

_____

_____

_____

_____

_____

_____

_____

_____

_____

_____

Knocking Down Strongholds

"I use God's mighty weapons, not those made
by men, to knock down the devil's strongholds."

2 Corinthians 10:4 (TLB)

One of my favorite scenes in the movie
"Black Panther" is when the sister/princess is
showing her brother all of the new
technology and weapons that they can use
to fight their enemies. They needed to
protect themselves from those who wanted
to take their vital resources and use them for
their own purposes. In the spiritual fight that
we are in, we have to do the same thing and
that is use the weapons that God provides to
fight the enemy of our soul. God's weapons
are tried and true. They work to knock down
the devil's strongholds.

Although, he may think that he has a
stronghold on you, it is only temporary,
God's weapons always work.

God doesn't change, but His methods, strategies and weapons can change all of the time. Sometimes, He tells you to be quiet, and other times, you have to shout. Sometimes, He tells you to use a rock and a rag, and others times, it's a song and crying. But no matter the weapon, the stronghold will be knocked down.

REFLECTION

_____

_____

_____

_____

_____

_____

_____

_____

_____

_____

_____

_____

_____

_____

_____

_____

_____

_____

_____

_____

_____

_____

REFLECTION

_____

_____

_____

_____

_____

_____

_____

_____

_____

_____

_____

_____

_____

_____

_____

_____

_____

_____

_____

_____

_____

Knock It Down

"But Jesus said, "The time is coming when all these things you are admiring will be knocked down, and not one stone will be left on top of another; all will become one vast heap of rubble."

Luke 21:6 (MSG)

I confess that there have been people whom I have admired and been in the same room with to hopefully, gain some influence but, God said no. I was disappointed, but now I understand. He told me that any level of success that I obtained would be because of Him and Him alone. He may use others to assist in some way, shape or form, but the glory will all be God's.

The children of Israel were admiring and probably half worshipping a building, the temple and something that they built with their own hands. Jesus said, "What you're admiring will be knocked down and not one stone will be on top of each other." That sounds like destruction to me. A complete demolishing. If God said it, it will happen, and it did. I don't believe that admiration of anything is a sin, but when you put it before God, He will demolish it or you may be disappointed by it and realize that it wasn't worth that amount of time, attention or admiration.

Don't let God Knock it over.

REFLECTION

_____
_____
_____
_____
_____
_____
_____
_____
_____
_____
_____
_____
_____
_____
_____
_____
_____
_____
_____
_____
_____
_____
_____

REFLECTION

_____
_____
_____
_____
_____
_____
_____
_____
_____
_____
_____
_____
_____
_____
_____
_____
_____
_____
_____
_____
_____
_____

Rhoda Get the Door

"He knocked at the door in the gate, and a girl named Rhoda came to open it."

Acts 12:13 (NLT)

In ancient times, they didn't have a doorbell, so people actually knocked on the door. The people had been praying for Peter's release from prison. The authorities had threatened that Peter would be killed for preaching Jesus. The church went into fervent prayer and supplication for Peter's release.

The knock came at the door. A young girl named Rhoda was asked to open the door. Can you imagine being asked such a simple task but realizing that the one act could be the miracle that you have praying so hard for?

Obedience is still great sacrifice and sometimes, it is just the smallest acts that bring the miracle, the answer or the deliverance to you. Rhoda wasn't asked to pay hundreds of dollars, perform weeks of antics or sacrifice her morals or standards but just to do a daily, routine and ordinary task of walking to the door and opening the door for whoever was standing on the other side of the door.

Your answer may be knocking but, like Rhoda, go get the door.

REFLECTION

_____

_____

_____

_____

_____

_____

_____

_____

_____

_____

_____

_____

_____

_____

_____

_____

_____

_____

_____

_____

_____

_____

_____

_____

REFLECTION

_____

_____

_____

_____

_____

_____

_____

_____

_____

_____

_____

_____

_____

_____

_____

_____

_____

_____

_____

_____

_____

The Answer is at the Door

"Meanwhile, Peter continued knocking. When they finally went out and opened the door, their surprise knew no bounds."

Acts 12:16 (NLT)

Peter, the answer to their prayers, continued to knock on the door. Why, because they felt like the most important thing for them was to pray. Until the answer comes, that is the most important thing, but when there is a knock at the door, you stay in a prayerful mode and answer the door.

There are some answers that only come when you open the door. Some answers at the door don't always look like what you thought so you slam the door in the answer's face.

Rhoda was in such shock that when she opened the door and Peter was standing there, she shut the door and ran to tell everyone that Peter was at the door.

The answer to their prayers was standing there at the door, but because of the shock, the door was closed and Peter had to start knocking again.

Rhoda, answer the door and keep the door open, because the answer is at the door.

REFLECTION

_____

_____

_____

_____

_____

_____

_____

_____

_____

_____

_____

_____

_____

_____

_____

_____

_____

_____

_____

_____

REFLECTION

_____
_____
_____
_____
_____
_____
_____
_____
_____
_____
_____
_____
_____
_____
_____
_____
_____
_____
_____
_____
_____
_____

Knocked Down but God is with Me

"We are hunted down, but God never abandons us. We get knocked down, but we get up again and keep going."

2 Corinthians 4:9 (LTB)

At my age, falling down is painful and the healing and recovery process will take much longer. God forbid, I sprain something or break something that will increase the recovery time. In this scripture, we don't accidentally fall down; we are literally being knocked down.

Now, being knocked down is when someone has strategically and intentionally waited, watched your patterns and timed it perfectly to knock you down. Now, I am a big girl so that would take a lot in the physical realm.

But let's talk about the spiritual, professional or business realm of things.

There are people who plot, plan and execute their plans to not only knock you down, which is temporary, but they want to knock you out, destroy you and eliminate you from coming back from the knock down.

With God, we may get knocked down, but we WILL get back up. No matter the bruises, bumps, rest, medicine and recovery time, we will get back up. Why? Because God is with us and we shall NOT fail.

REFLECTION

_____

_____

_____

_____

_____

_____

_____

_____

_____

_____

_____

_____

_____

_____

_____

_____

_____

_____

_____

_____

_____

_____

REFLECTION

_____
_____
_____
_____
_____
_____
_____
_____
_____
_____
_____
_____
_____
_____
_____
_____
_____
_____
_____
_____
_____
_____
_____

Just Knock, the Door will Open

"Everyone who asks, receives; all who seek, find; and the door is opened to everyone who knocks."

Luke 11:10 (NLT)

The beauty of this scripture and promise starts at the beginning, with "everyone." Because everyone who asks, receives everyone seeks will find and the door will open to everyone who knocks.

What a promise. What a guarantee. What a consequence of an action. What a cause that makes you want to ask, seek and knock.

The problem that I find with people is that they stand in front of, speak to or signal for someone else to do the knocking when it is a requirement for them to knock so the door will open. Some people love for the door to be opened for them. My husband opens the door for me often and I enjoy it. But that's not this type of door because what is behind this door may not be meant for the door holder but just the door opener.

If you are knocking on a door that is prepared for you and you are prepared for it, you don't really want anybody else to open that door because sometimes somebody else will take the credit for the door, the opening and what is behind the door.

If you are independent, like me, I appreciate all that you did, said, assisted me, pointed me in the right direction, encouraged me to go for it, but there are some doors I have to knock on myself and watch God open it for me.

REFLECTION

_____

_____
_____
_____
_____
_____
_____
_____
_____
_____
_____
_____
_____
_____
_____
_____
_____
_____
_____
_____
_____
_____
_____
_____
_____

REFLECTION

_____
_____
_____
_____
_____
_____
_____
_____
_____
_____
_____
_____
_____
_____
_____
_____
_____
_____
_____
_____
_____
_____

Ready to Open the Door

"...for your Lord's return from the wedding feast. Then you will be ready to open the door and let him in the moment he arrives and knocks."

Luke 12:36 (NLT)

Are you ready to open the door when Jesus Himself knocks. The Lord will return to the sky to prepare for the wedding feast with the Bride of Christ and we on earth must be ready to the open the door and let the Bridegroom in when He knocks on the door.

My mother is one that if you say that you are coming to pick her up at 11:00 a.m., she is sitting by the door or near the door fully dressed with coat and hat on with the cane in one hand and her purse in the other at 10:00 a.m. She is normally not getting ready but ready to walk out the door when you pull into her driveway. That's the way she taught us to be when riding with someone else, and I am still doing that to this day.

The Lord is not giving us a time, day nor hour when He is coming, just be ready to open the door when He knocks by blowing the trumpet and says, "Come my people."

REFLECTION

REFLECTION

_____

_____

_____

_____

_____

_____

_____

_____

_____

_____

_____

_____

_____

_____

_____

_____

_____

_____

_____

_____

Don't Open the Door to a Stranger

"The door to heaven is narrow. Work hard to get in, for the truth is that many will try to enter, but when the head of the house has locked the door, it will be too late. Then, if you stand outside knocking and pleading, 'Lord, open the door for us,' he will reply, 'I do not know you.'"

Luke 13:24-25 (TLB)

The historic 'Little Richard' song was 'keep a knockin' but you can't come in.' Now, I don't know who he was talking about, but the Lord has the key, the door and no matter how long or how hard you try to get in, the door won't open. Also, in Luke, when asked to open the door, Jesus says, "I don't know you."

That is rule #1 of safety in any home to not open the door for people you don't know. If you look through the peephole or pull back the curtain and you don't know them, call your parents to come to the door.

It's dangerous to open the door to a stranger. But with God's power, nobody is getting in the door of Heaven or your heart without Him knowing about it.

Be ready to open the door to the Father. Definitely don't open the door to a stranger. Keep knocking, but you, ma'am or sir, will not get in.

REFLECTION

REFLECTION

_____
_____
_____
_____
_____
_____
_____
_____
_____
_____
_____
_____
_____
_____
_____
_____
_____
_____
_____
_____
_____
_____
_____

My Beloved is Knocking

"I sleep, but my heart waketh: it is the voice of my beloved that knocketh."

Song of Solomon 5:2 (KJV)

My father loved to entertain his family. He bought more food, soft drinks and desserts than we were ever going to eat. Why? He loved family time. The more people who came in the driveway, the louder and happier he got. He would ask the neighbors if they would be home or if we could park some cars in their driveway. On the holidays, they would pull their cars in their garage and the driveway was ours. He would yell, "Come on in!" My mother would yell as well, "There they are!" Let the party begin.

There is something about when someone is knocking at your door that you love or that you want to see or that in this scripture says, 'your heart wakes up' because you hear their voice and see them. 'My beloved knocketh' is not just anybody ordinary who is knocking on the door like the mailman or someone soliciting, but it's someone you love deeply and they are very important to your life. They have been with you through many heartaches and triumphs, sickness and health but also failure and success.

Who is knocking on the door? It's my beloved. Open that door and make it quick.

REFLECTION

_____
_____
_____
_____
_____
_____
_____
_____
_____
_____
_____
_____
_____
_____
_____
_____
_____
_____
_____
_____
_____
_____
_____
_____
_____
_____
_____
_____

REFLECTION

_____

_____

_____

_____

_____

_____

_____

_____

_____

_____

_____

_____

_____

_____

_____

_____

_____

_____

_____

_____

_____

_____

He Knocked Over the Tables

"When they arrived back in Jerusalem, He went to the Temple and began to drive out the merchants and their customers, and knocked over the tables of the money changers and the stalls of those selling doves..."

Mark 11:15 (TLB)

I confess that I am clumsy. I have bumped into things, spilled a whole glass of water on a table and actually fallen while going upstairs, not downstairs, but upstairs. I missed the step, didn't look down or was going too fast and fell down. Ouch! Yes, it hurt.

Jesus, was displeased with the excessive and merchandising in the Temple. It was necessary to have a gift, an offering or something in your hand when you came into the Temple, but it had gotten out of hand.

The Temple had turned into a marketplace and not the sanctuary for prayer and worship to God. They were not outside of the gates prior to entering into the Temple but actually inside. It had become a distraction and took the focus away from God. Money answereth all things, but God is still number one, the purpose for church, and He is to be honored at all times.

Jesus' anger made Him knock over and turn over the tables. It wasn't an accident; He wasn't being clumsy but very intentional about His actions. "My house shall be a house of prayer." That's the focus. That's the goal. The reason for the Temple was prayer and worship unto God.

Don't let God knock over your table.

REFLECTION

_____
_____
_____
_____
_____
_____
_____
_____
_____
_____
_____
_____
_____
_____
_____
_____
_____
_____
_____
_____
_____

REFLECTION

_____
_____
_____
_____
_____
_____
_____
_____
_____
_____
_____
_____
_____
_____
_____
_____
_____
_____
_____
_____
_____
_____

Knocked Down by a demon, You Will Get Back Up!

"As the boy was coming, the demon knocked him to the ground and threw him into a violent convulsion. But Jesus ordered the demon to come out and healed the boy and handed him over to his father."

Luke 9:42 (NLT)

One thing about it, and two things, for sure, if you ever get knocked down, you won't stay down in the presence of Jesus. This story is one of a family that has a troubled and sick child. He needed to be healed internally and mentally from the demonic forces that were tormenting him.

The parents came to Jesus and described all of the things that the spirits caused him to do and the child couldn't even live at home. The boy lived in the cemetery, cutting himself and often times, had been thrown into the fire. But after the demon knocked the child to the ground, Jesus showed up, healed the boy, and he was able to go home with his parents.

What has the enemy knocked you down from or seeking to actually knock you out of and from? Just like in any fight, the knock down doesn't always mean a knock out.

The power of Jesus can heal you and help you to overcome the enemy, rather than the enemy overpowering you. I believe in Jesus and doctors to assist with the healing and recovery process.

With God you shall recover all.

REFLECTION

REFLECTION

The Persistent Knock

"But I'll tell you this—though He won't do it as a
friend, if you keep knocking long enough, He
will get up and give you everything you want—
just because of your persistence."

Luke 11:8 (NLT)

As someone who coaches people to start
businesses, one of the biggest problems is
not capital, start-up money or a good
product or service, but persistence. The first
sign of trouble, resistance, or a no, the
person wants to quick, give up and throw in
the towel.

I can tell you now that I wanted to quit and
the budget said I should quit in the first five
years of business. But I was persistent. I
changed some things. I learned some more
things. I got a coach. I took some courses. I
learned some more strategies, studied
people online, in person, and on-demand
courses, but I kept going and didn't quit. I
persistently kept knocking on that literary
business door until it opened, and I gained

access to clients and grew my business to sustain itself for now 17+ years. The first no or not now or I don't have the money or I went with another publisher was disappointing, but there are 8 billion people on the planet. If I keep writing, learning from others, showcasing my work and getting in front of the right audiences, somebody will do business with me.

Are you consistent and persistent? Do you give up easily and lose your momentum? The persistent person who keeps knocking is going to one day see that door swing open wide and be ready for the opportunity on the other side. Keep knocking...

REFLECTION

REFLECTION

_____
_____
_____
_____
_____
_____
_____
_____
_____
_____
_____
_____
_____
_____
_____
_____
_____
_____
_____
_____
_____

For Everyone

"For every one that asketh receiveth; and he that seeketh findeth; and to him that knocketh it shall be opened."

Matthew 7:8 (KJV)

— ❧❧ ❧❧ —

There are some things in life that are NOT for everyone. Everyone is an individual and has the very right to like, do and act the way they want. Even God has made us free moral agents. We are free to choose, decide and act on the decisions that we've made. You are different from me. I am unique and my fingerprint says so. We can agree to disagree. We can never agree on the same things and I can still love you.

But this is a strong scripture in that it starts out 'for everyone.' Whatever comes after 'for everyone', is an opportunity, law and/or a promise. 'For everyone' means you and you and you too. It doesn't leave anyone out. No matter what you look like, where you come from, who your family is and how much money you make, it's still for you. Have you ever gotten a gift and the wrapping was pretty but in the back of your mind you're wondering, *what did we get?*

That is what I'm thinking about after the words 'for everyone,' what did we get? We get to receive if we ask. We will find it if we seek, and if there is a door, it will open if we knock. The opportunity IS for everyone, but there is still something that you have to do, BUT if you do it, it will happen for you too. Remember, it's for everyone.

REFLECTION

_____
_____
_____
_____
_____
_____
_____
_____
_____
_____
_____
_____
_____
_____
_____
_____
_____
_____
_____
_____

REFLECTION

_____

_____

_____

_____

_____

_____

_____

_____

_____

_____

_____

_____

_____

_____

_____

_____

_____

_____

_____

_____

_____

God Showed Out

"Therefore, I make this decree, that any person of any nation, language, or religion who speaks a word against the God of Shadrach, Meshach, and Abednego shall be torn limb from limb and his house knocked into a heap of rubble. For no other God can do what this one does."

Daniel 3:29 (TLB)

There are some people who may start out as your enemy but will change their minds after the incident. You know the incident. They threatened you, spoke negatively about you, your dreams, goals, business or family. You didn't retaliate. You didn't defend yourself but kept moving, working and striving to do what you are supposed to do. In this life, everyone is not going to like you or agree with you.

The young men in this very familiar biblical story had been threatened by a king because they wouldn't worship him or his idol god. In captivity, they worshipped Jehovah God. The decree was sent out, but these three young men kept their routine of worship to Jehovah and stood up when the others bowed to the idol god.

The threat was carried out, but God, Jehovah, showed up for them and 'showed out.' Jehovah delivered the young men out of the fiery furnace, and as a result, the king said, "Whoever comes against these young men's God, Jehovah, I'm going to tear you from limb to limb and knock your house down into a heap of rubble or pile of stones."

What a testimony. What a turn of events. When your enemy recognizes your God and is now threatening others for not recognizing the power of your God. What a mighty God we serve. Show up and show out God. The enemy is watching.

REFLECTION

_____
_____
_____
_____
_____
_____
_____
_____
_____
_____
_____
_____
_____
_____
_____
_____
_____
_____
_____
_____
_____
_____

REFLECTION

_____

_____

_____

_____

_____

_____

_____

_____

_____

_____

_____

_____

_____

_____

_____

_____

_____

_____

_____

_____

_____

_____

Handwriting on the Wall

"His face blanched with fear, and such terror
gripped him that his knees knocked together
and his legs gave way beneath him."

Daniel 5:6 (TLB)

Some biblical sayings are very common in the modern world today. "I was shaking in my boots" or "I saw the handwriting on the wall" are two very common sayings.

In Daniel, the king ruler at the time didn't believe in Jehovah God. He had power, control and wanted to invoke his power on everyone in his kingdom. It was his right, but it wasn't right. The warning came for him to stop in the form of an invisible hand writing a message to him on his own wall. Pause for a second and realize that no one is untouchable and void of receiving a message from God. God will change His methods to get His message across to anyone. The invisible hand writing on the king's wall was so powerful that his knees knocked together and he couldn't stand because of the inability of his knees and legs to hold him.

Not only was he in fear, but terror. The root word for terrorist is terror. Terror is a level that goes beyond fear. Your power and control do not stand up to the terrorist and they take over, do what they will and control your atmosphere and environment.

Adding insult to injury, God wrote the message in a way that only Daniel could interpret it. The people that this king was terrorizing were the same people that he needed their help to stop his own terror. God is something else.

The message is clear. The handwriting is on the wall. Act accordingly. God is speaking.

REFLECTION

REFLECTION

_____
_____
_____
_____
_____
_____
_____
_____
_____
_____
_____
_____
_____
_____
_____
_____
_____
_____
_____
_____
_____

Eye for an Eye

"If her eye is injured, injure his; if her tooth is knocked out, knock out his; and so on—hand for hand, foot for foot."

Exodus 21:24 (TLB)

If we acted out everything they did in the ancient biblical times today, there would be a lot of people with missing limbs and vital organs. If someone knocked out a tooth or eye from you or your servant, you could literally go to them and knock out their tooth or eye or their servant's tooth or eye. That's where the saying 'an eye for an eye' comes from. That was the Old Testament activity. In the New Testament, Jesus says, "Turn the other cheek and do not seek to get revenge on your enemy."

Today, there are some people who seek and do physical harm to people as a form of revenge. The gangs in the streets are notorious for senseless murders of people as a form of revenge. It's normally over territory, street corners and/or ability to move merchandise. Others may not seek to do bodily harm, but they want to knock out your peace and ability to sleep at night for the gossip and negative talk about you. Some people seek revenge by knocking out your ability to get a promotion, access to the resources that you need to just better yourself and your family. Some people see your success as a threat. Don't seek your own revenge. Don't follow the 'eye for an eye' revenge methods.

God said, "Vengeance is mine and I will repay."

By the way, I need both of my eyes.

REFLECTION

_____

_____

_____

_____

_____

_____

_____

_____

_____

_____

_____

_____

_____

_____

_____

_____

_____

_____

_____

_____

REFLECTION

_____
_____
_____
_____
_____
_____
_____
_____
_____
_____
_____
_____
_____
_____
_____
_____
_____
_____
_____
_____
_____
_____
_____

Knocked it Down

"He also went to Penuel and knocked down the city tower and killed the entire male population."

Judges 8:17 (TLB)

A promise is a promise. The story of Gideon with only 300 men doing God's will up against an army of more than 15,000. They came to a city and asked for help along the way. All they needed was some food to strengthen them because they were tired from chasing and tracking the enemy. In ancient times, hospitality was a sign of a civilized city. Entertaining strangers, providing the basic necessities of food and water, was the norm. This city said, "Nope, can't help you." Sometimes, when you receive a 'no', let that be the fuel to energize your mission. That's what Gideon used this 'no' to do for him and his army. It was the fuel and he left hungry and tired but with a promise. I'll be back.

You'd think that with 300 men, it would be easy to track 15,000, but it wasn't. The enemy was strong and fast, but Gideon was determined. He had a word from God brought by an angel to do a job, and he was going to finish it.

When the town's leaders refused to feed or help Gideon and his army, he told them, "After I complete this mission, I'll be back to finish you and knock down this tower." I'm quite sure that they didn't believe Gideon, but it happened just like he said. He pursued, overtook and destroyed his initial enemy and then came back to this city and knocked down their tower, and it killed all of the men of the city.

You promised yourself and others, so knock it down. Knock down that list of things that you have to do. Knock down that debt so you can be financially free. Knock down that doubt so that you move forward and live that BEST life. Knock it down.

REFLECTION

_____

_____

_____

_____

_____

_____

_____

_____

_____

_____

_____

_____

_____

_____

_____

_____

_____

_____

_____

_____

_____

_____

REFLECTION

_____
_____
_____
_____
_____
_____
_____
_____
_____
_____
_____
_____
_____
_____
_____
_____
_____
_____
_____
_____

The People Did It

"The king appointed his special assistant to control the traffic at the gate, but he was knocked down and trampled and killed as the people rushed out. This is what Elisha had predicted on the previous day when the king had come to arrest him."

2 Kings 7:17 (NLT)

One prophet, one person who was a doubter, but a lot of people helped to fulfill the prophecy. Have you ever received a word from a prophet that you may or may not have believed and it actually came true? The beauty of God is that He will sometimes use people who never heard the prophecy, didn't know that they were key players in its fulfillment and acted on God's command without knowing that God was using them. The prophet prophesied it and the people did it. The special assistant of the king was trying to control traffic, slow the people down from getting what the prophet had prophesied, and because he was in the way, he got knocked down. Not only knocked down, but trampled to death.

God does not lie, keeps his promises and sometimes, He uses people to do it. Get in the way if you want to, but God's word will not be stopped or His promises fall to the ground not completed.

REFLECTION

REFLECTION

_____
_____
_____
_____
_____
_____
_____
_____
_____
_____
_____
_____
_____
_____
_____
_____
_____
_____
_____
_____
_____
_____
_____

No Idols Here

"He removed the shrines on the hills, broke down the obelisks, knocked down the shameful idols of Asherah, and broke up the bronze serpent that Moses had made, because the people of Israel had begun to worship it by burning incense to it; even though, as King Hezekiah pointed out to them, it was merely a piece of bronze."

2 Kings 18:4 (TLB)

Most of the time, people think of idols as something, some place or someone that you literally stop, drop to your knees or bow down and worship. An idol is anything that is put before the one true God. Sometimes, it's a thing, a car, a job, or a position. Other times, it is yourself, your ways, your thinking, your plans and dreams.

Whatever it is that interferes with God and His purpose for your life, you will find it removed, broken down, knocked down and/or broken up as in this text.

Whatever it takes, it must go. Sometimes, you don't even realize that you're worshipping it. Sometimes, you may think that you are just being a good steward of it, giving it the attention that it needs, but to God, it's too much and turns into idol worship.

There are doors that need to be knocked on so that they will open. There are some things that need to be knocked down so that doors can be opened to benefit your life.

REFLECTION

_____

_____

_____

_____

_____

_____

_____

_____

_____

_____

_____

_____

_____

_____

_____

_____

_____

_____

_____

_____

REFLECTION

_____
_____
_____
_____
_____
_____
_____
_____
_____
_____
_____
_____
_____
_____
_____
_____
_____
_____
_____
_____
_____
_____

It Was The Goat

"...The ram was powerless to stand against it; the goat knocked it to the ground and trampled on it, and none could rescue the ram from its power..."

Daniel 8:7 (NIV)

❧

The book of Daniel was filled with symbolism that we are still striving to unravel to this day. The prophet Daniel was a mighty man of God, used by God to warn His people, encourage them during captivity, but also to warn us, even to this day.

Besides the biblical significance is that the goat knocked down and trampled the ram. Now, physically and biologically, that's not normally the case. A goat can take out a sheep but not normally a ram. In the vision and prophecy, it was a goat taking out a ram. That's a warning and encouragement to all of us that sometimes God will use the less physically capable to overtake a much stronger and even larger enemy. No only did the goat knock down and trample the ram, but no one could rescue the ram from the power of the goat.

Now, I know that you are thinking, *I thought we were talking about knocking on doors*. But sometimes, the knocking is not only a door, but a thought, idea or doubt that is coming against the purpose and plan of God. Sometimes, it is a person, but no matter who or what is coming against you, know that you will defeat it and nobody will be able to rescue that enemy or force.

It was the goat that knocked it down.

REFLECTION

_____

_____

_____

_____

_____

_____

_____

_____

_____

_____

_____

_____

_____

_____

_____

_____

_____

_____

_____

_____

_____

REFLECTION

_____

_____

_____

_____

_____

_____

_____

_____

_____

_____

_____

_____

_____

_____

_____

_____

_____

_____

_____

_____

_____

_____

Don't Trust the Wall

"That nation will lay siege to your cities and knock down your highest walls—the walls you will trust to protect you."

Deuteronomy 28:52 (NLT)

There is a very famous traditional folksong titled, "Joshua Fit the Battle of Jericho." It goes on to say, "and the walls came tumbling down." This is taken directly from scripture referring to the children of Israel marching around the walls of Jericho seven times, seven days straight. Built and fortified walls, in ancient times, were a sign of power, prosperity and there was a strong army nearby ready to fight. You could seek refuge and protection in a walled city. Jericho's walls were so thick that it was said that two chariots could ride side by side around the walls. Truly, the sign of a secure and protected city.

But God warned the city that you can put your trust in those walls, but they will be knocked down. Not only any wall, but the highest wall will be knocked down. The highest wall is where the lookout, guard or sharpshooter was posted to take out the enemy even before they approached. The wall was usually too high to climb so that was a strategic place to destroy the enemy even before they got close.

You can strive to trust in those walls, but if God promised to knock it down, it's coming down.

Don't trust the walls.

REFLECTION

_____
_____
_____
_____
_____
_____
_____
_____
_____
_____
_____
_____
_____
_____
_____
_____
_____
_____
_____
_____
_____

REFLECTION

_____
_____
_____
_____
_____
_____
_____
_____
_____
_____
_____
_____
_____
_____
_____
_____
_____
_____
_____
_____
_____

About the Author

Julia Royston spends her days doing what she loves, writing, publishing, speaking about her why and motto, "Helping You Get Your Message to the Masses, Turn Your Words into Wealth and Be a Book Business Boss." Julia is the author of 140+ books, published 400+, recorded 3 music CDs and coached others to be published authors and business owners. She is the owner of five companies, a non-profit organization, and the editor of the Book Business Boss Magazine.

To stay connected with Julia, visit www.juliaakroyston.com.

Social Media

Facebook, Instagram, LinkedIn, TikTok
and Threads - @juliaaroyston

More Books by this Author

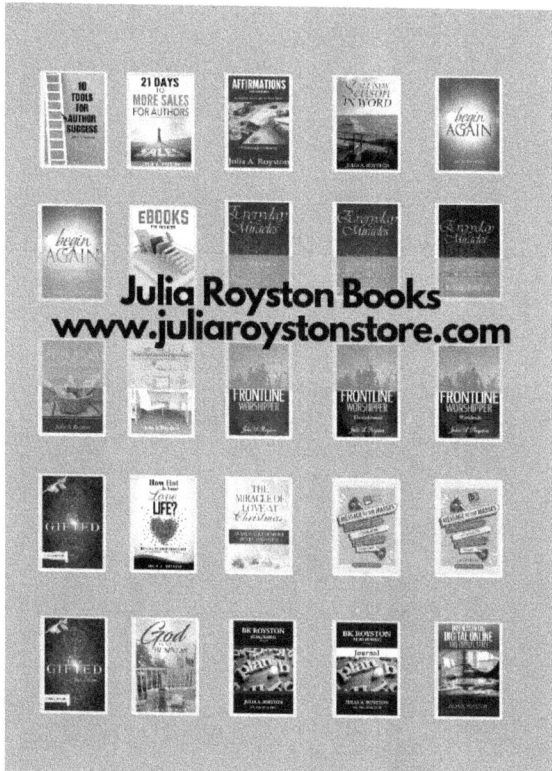

Julia Royston Books
www.juliaroystonstore.com

More Books by this Author

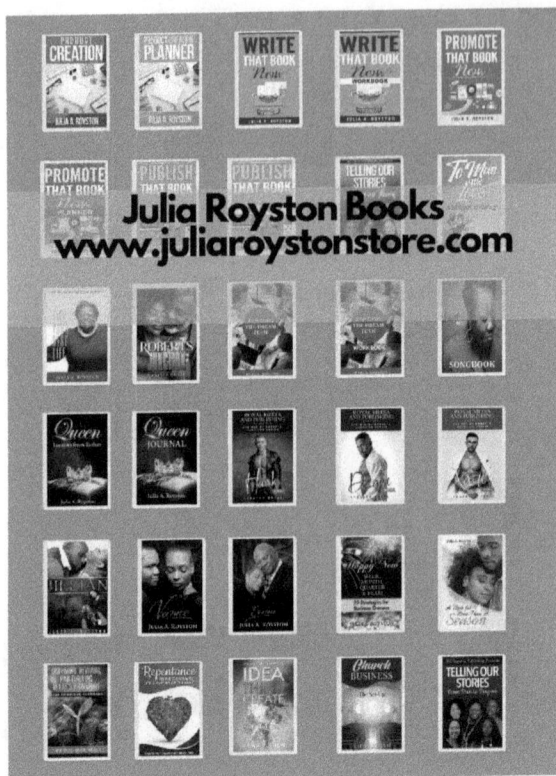

More Books by this Author

Julia Royston Books
www.juliaroystonstore.com

More Books by this Author

Julia Royston Books
www.juliaroystonstore.com

More Books by this Author

Julia Royston Books
www.roystonchildrenbookstore.com

More Books by this Author

Julia Royston Books
www.roystonchildrenbookstore.com

More Books by this Author

JOURNAL/SKETCHBOOKS

Julia Royston Books
www.roystonchildrenbookstore.com